Things I

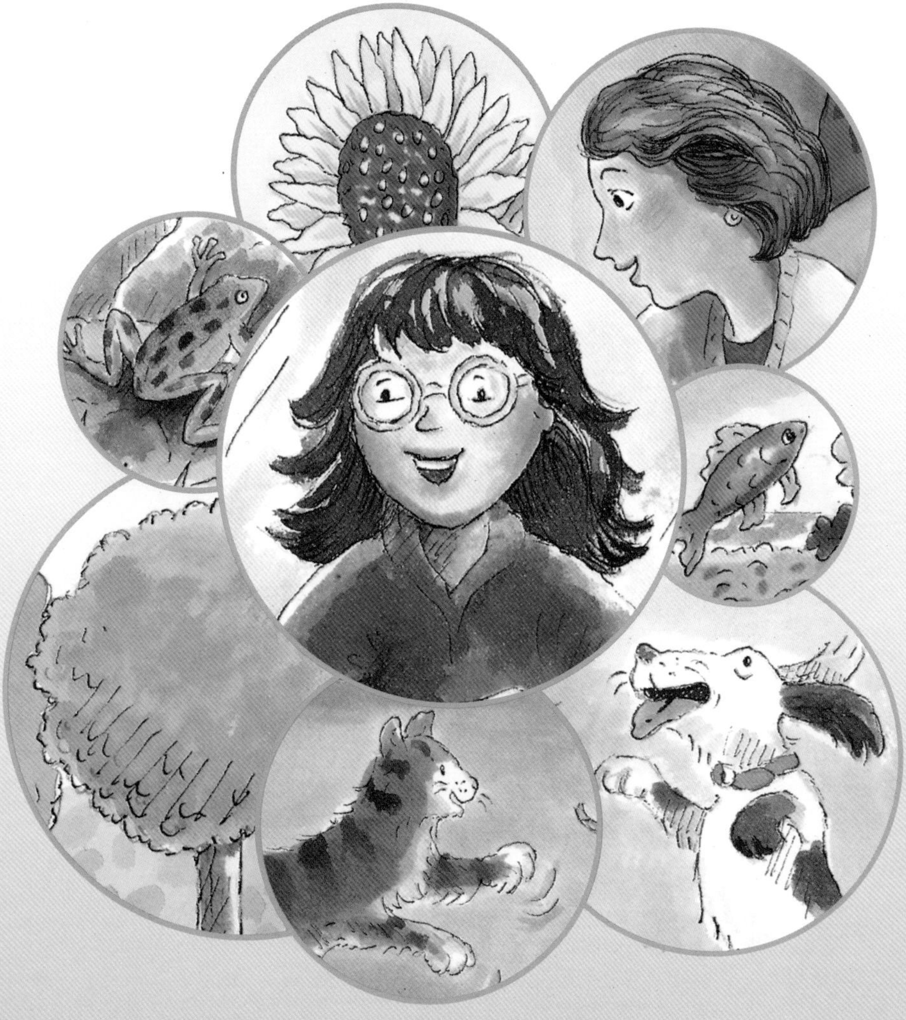

I like cats.

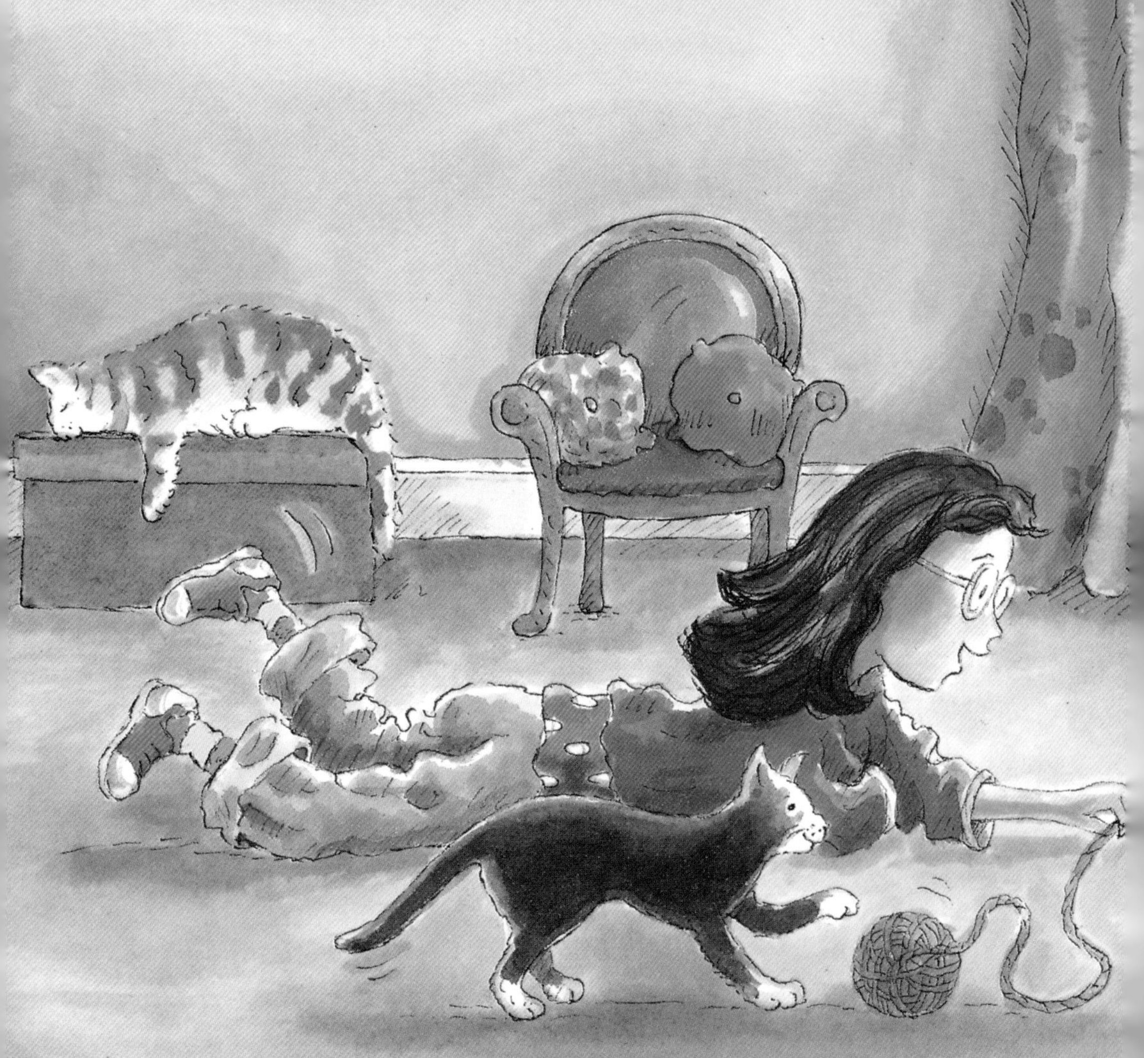

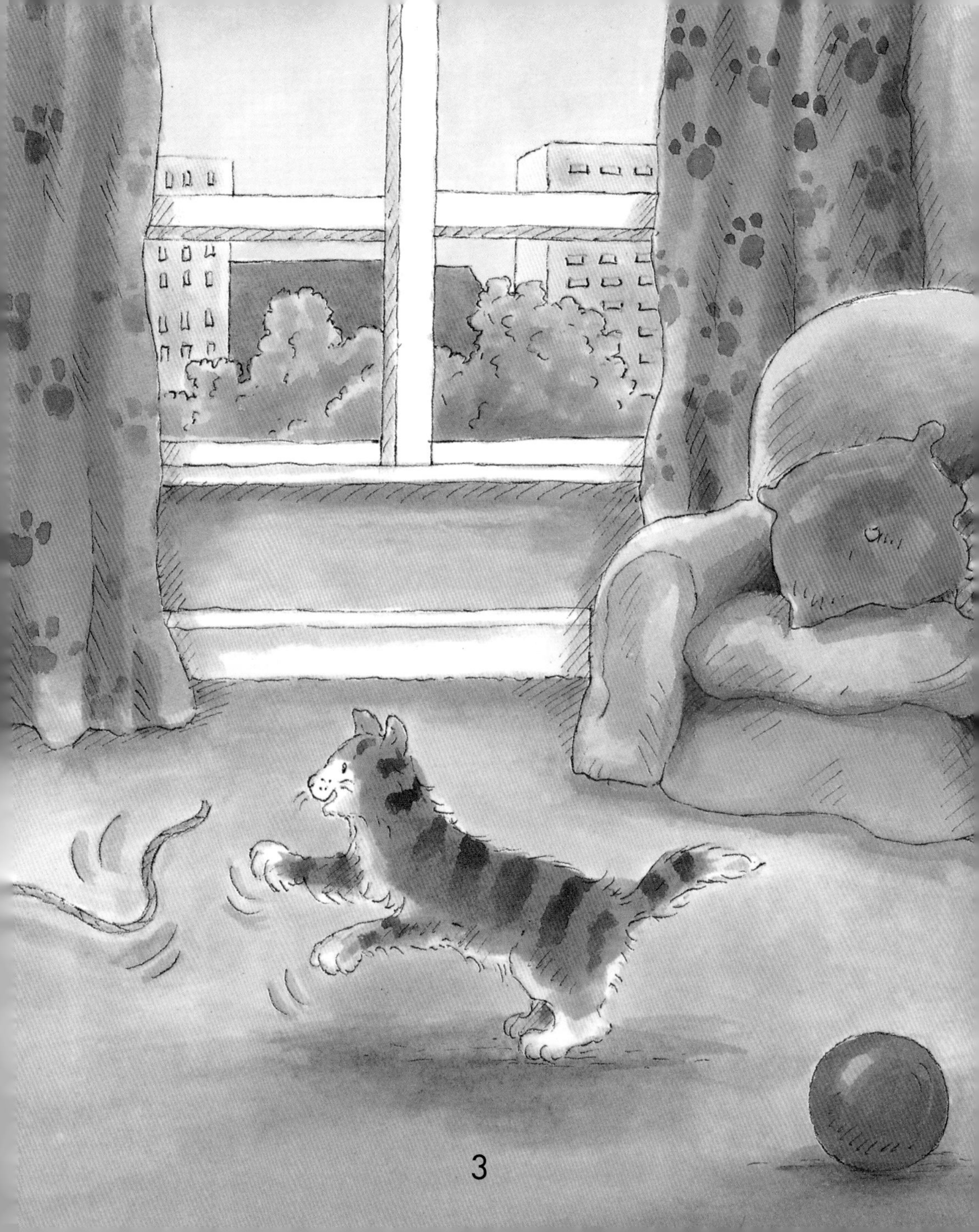

I like dogs.

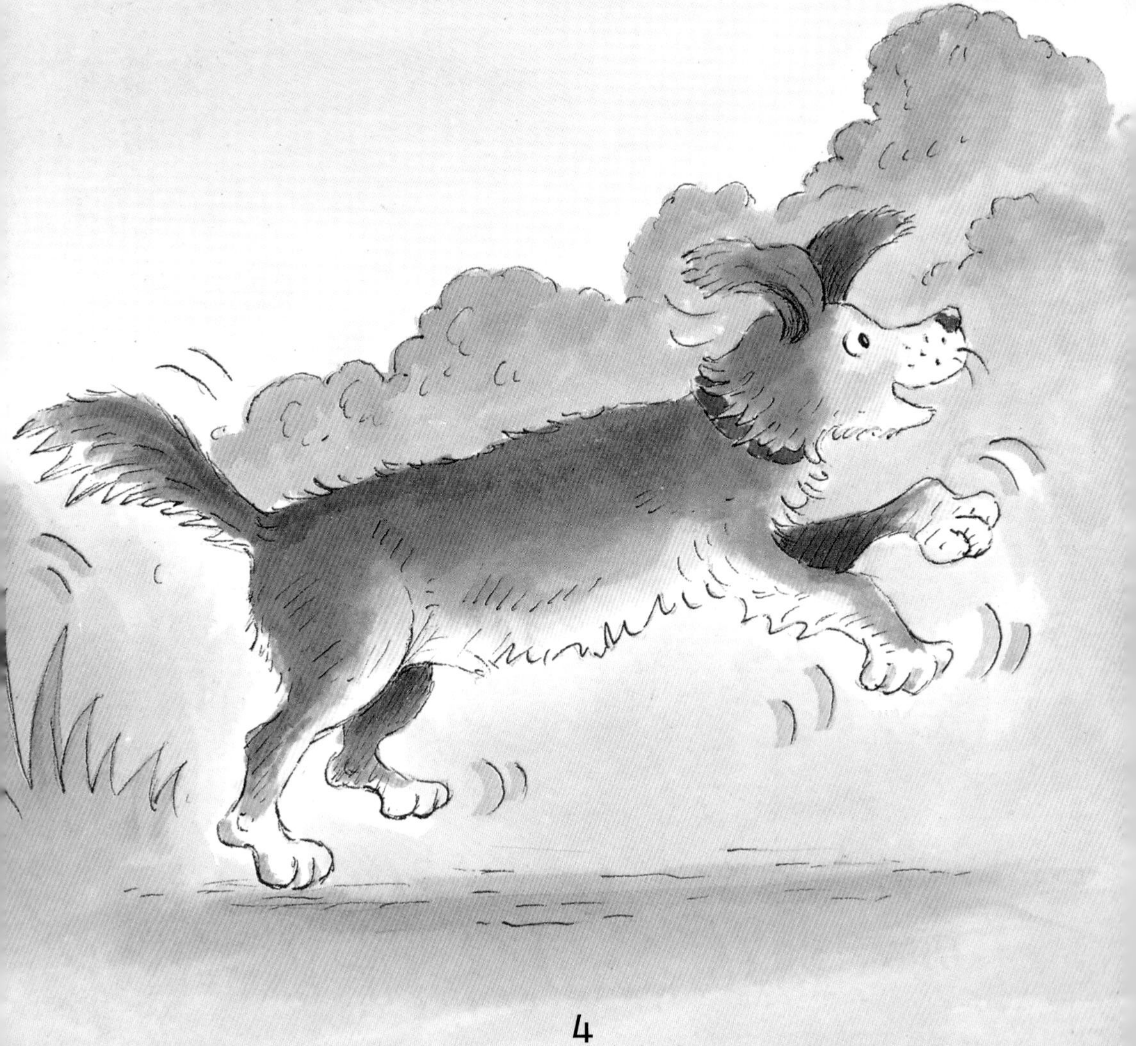

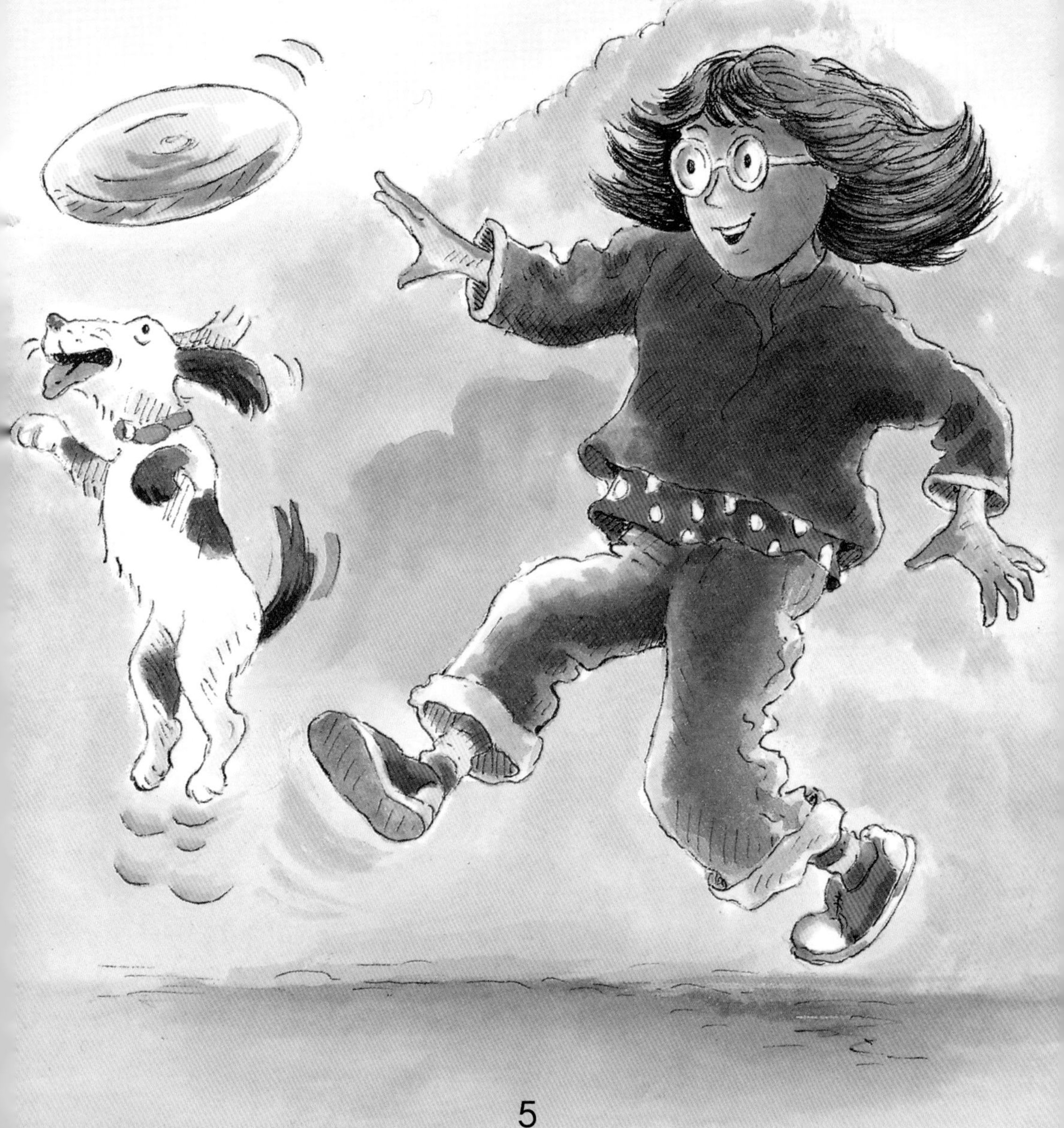

I like fish.

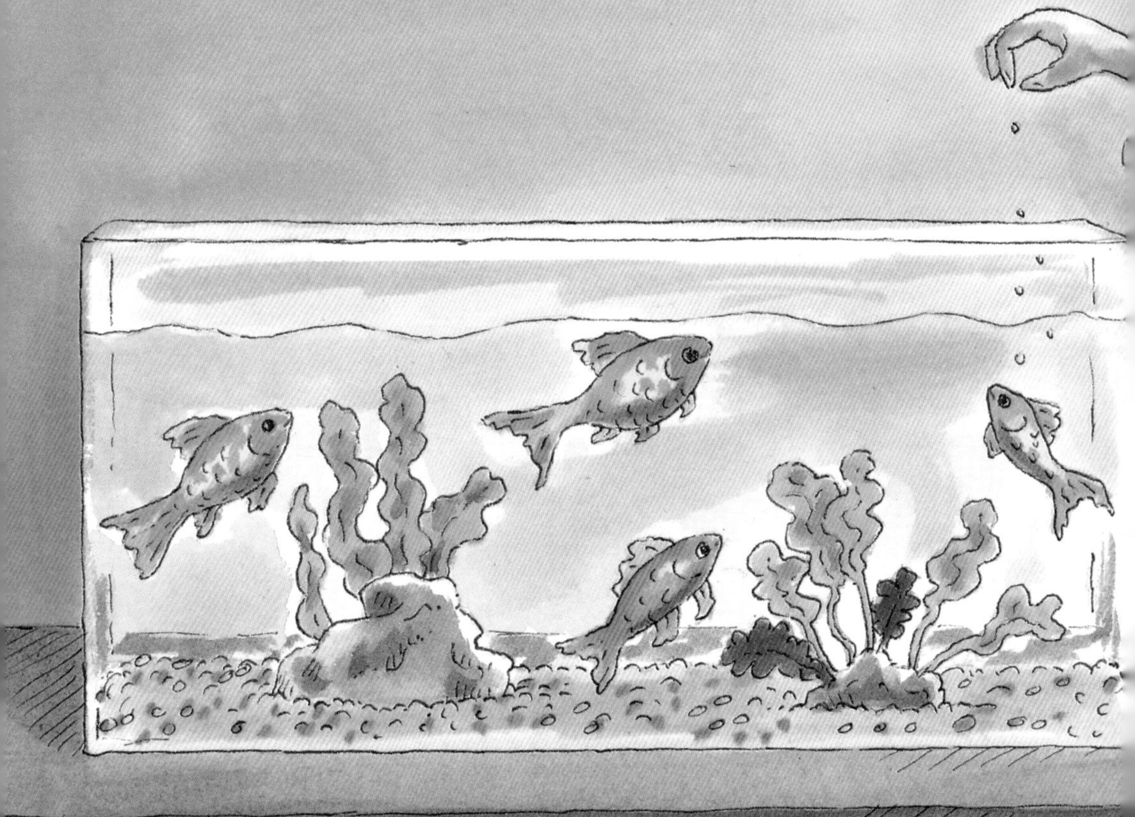

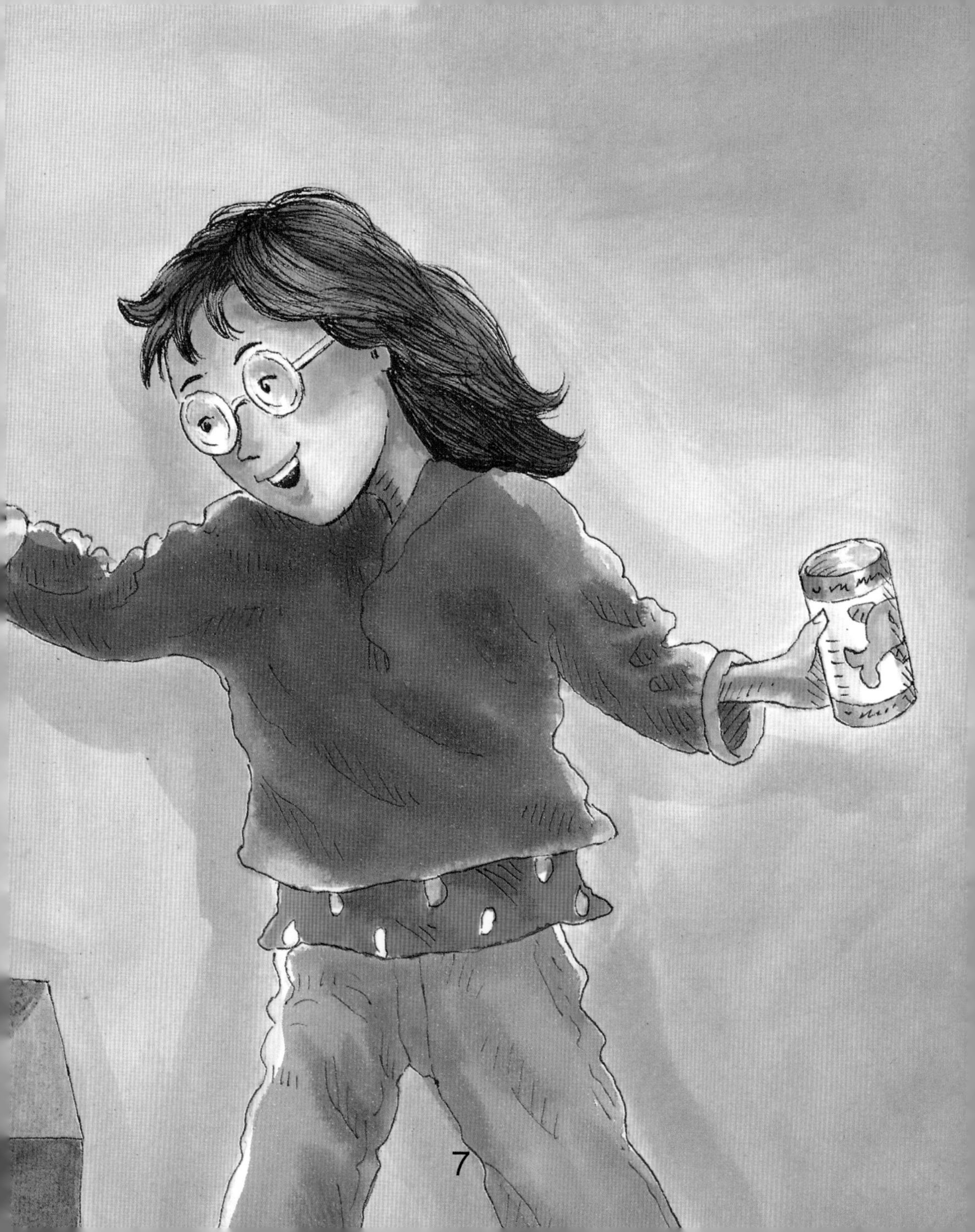

I like frogs.

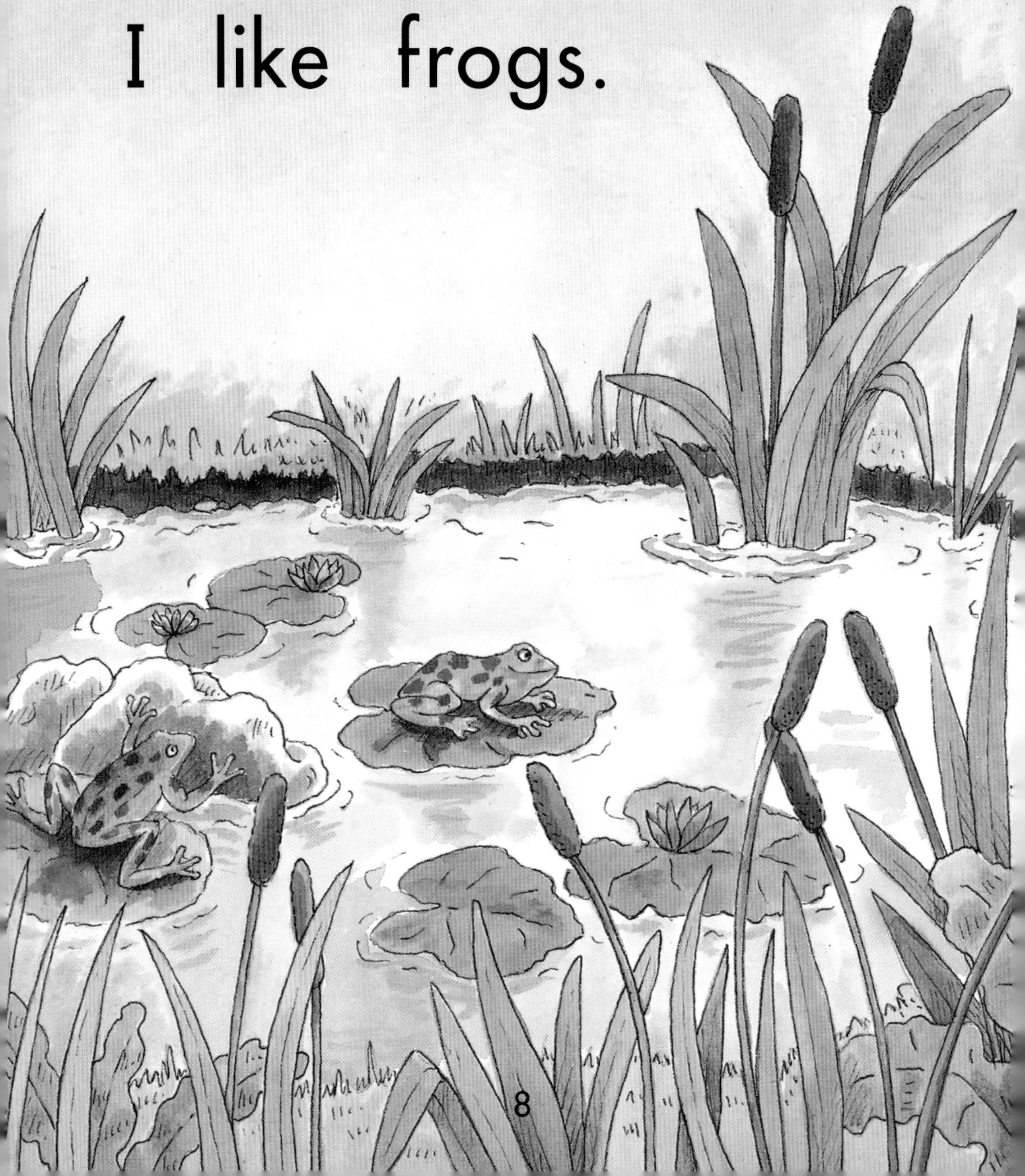

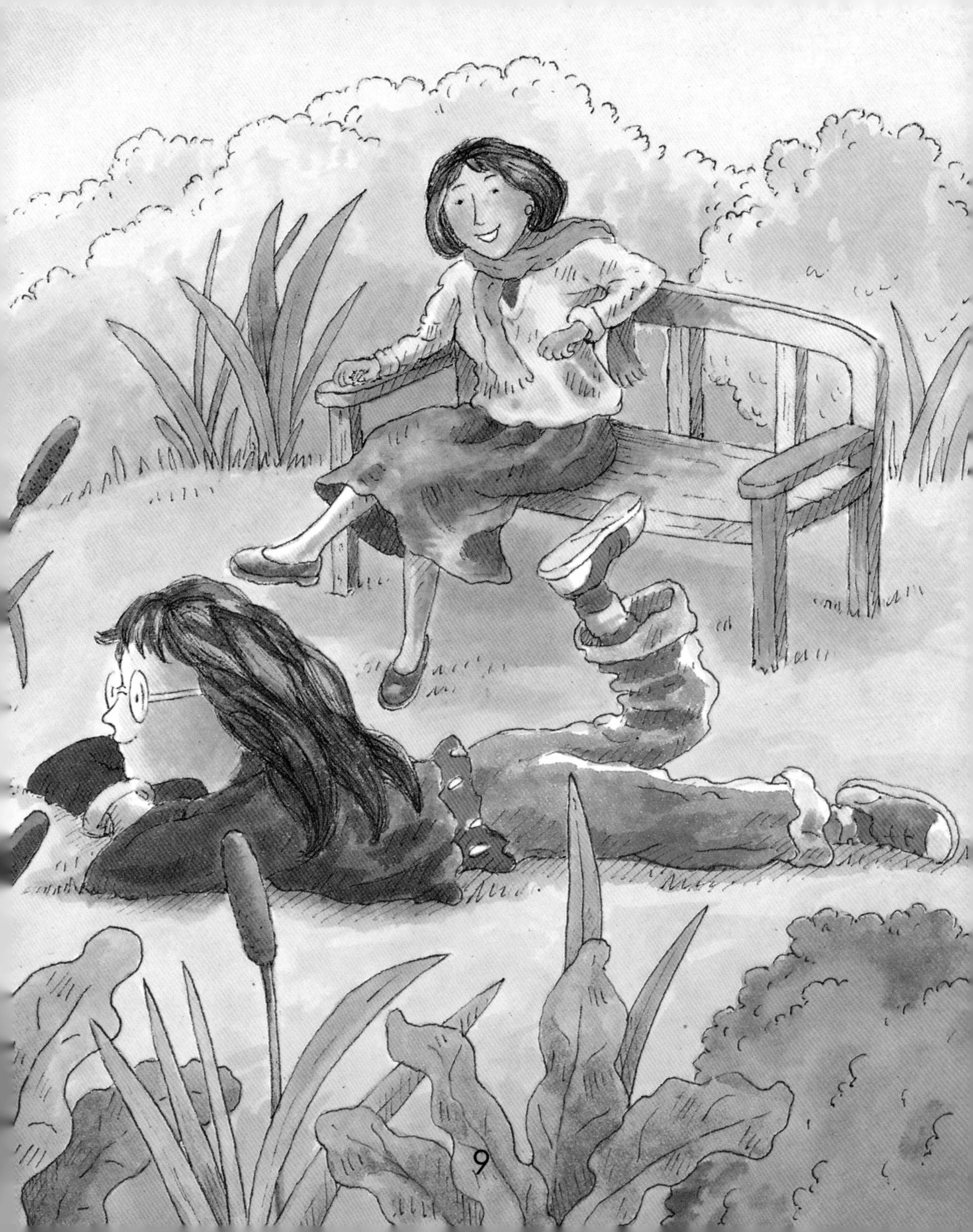

I like flowers.

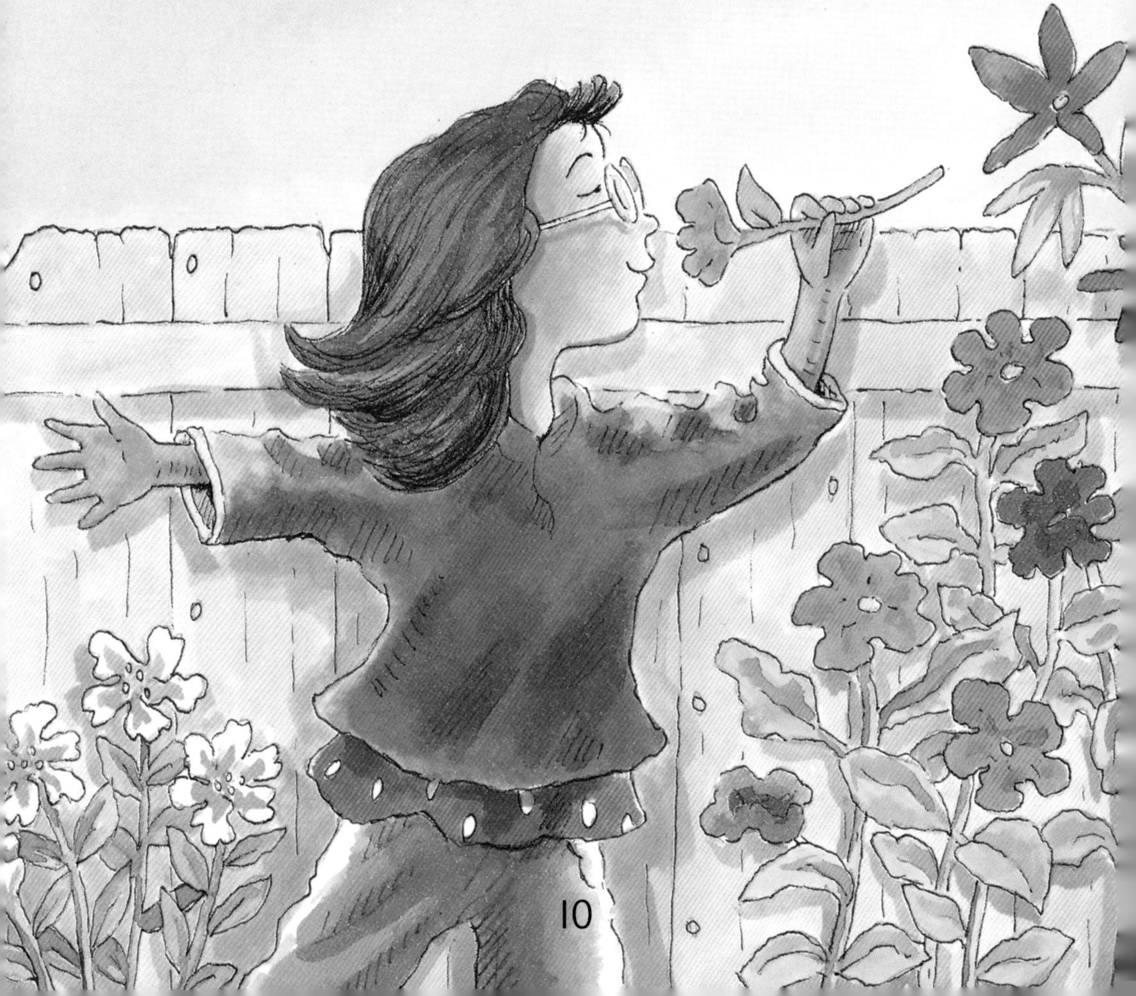

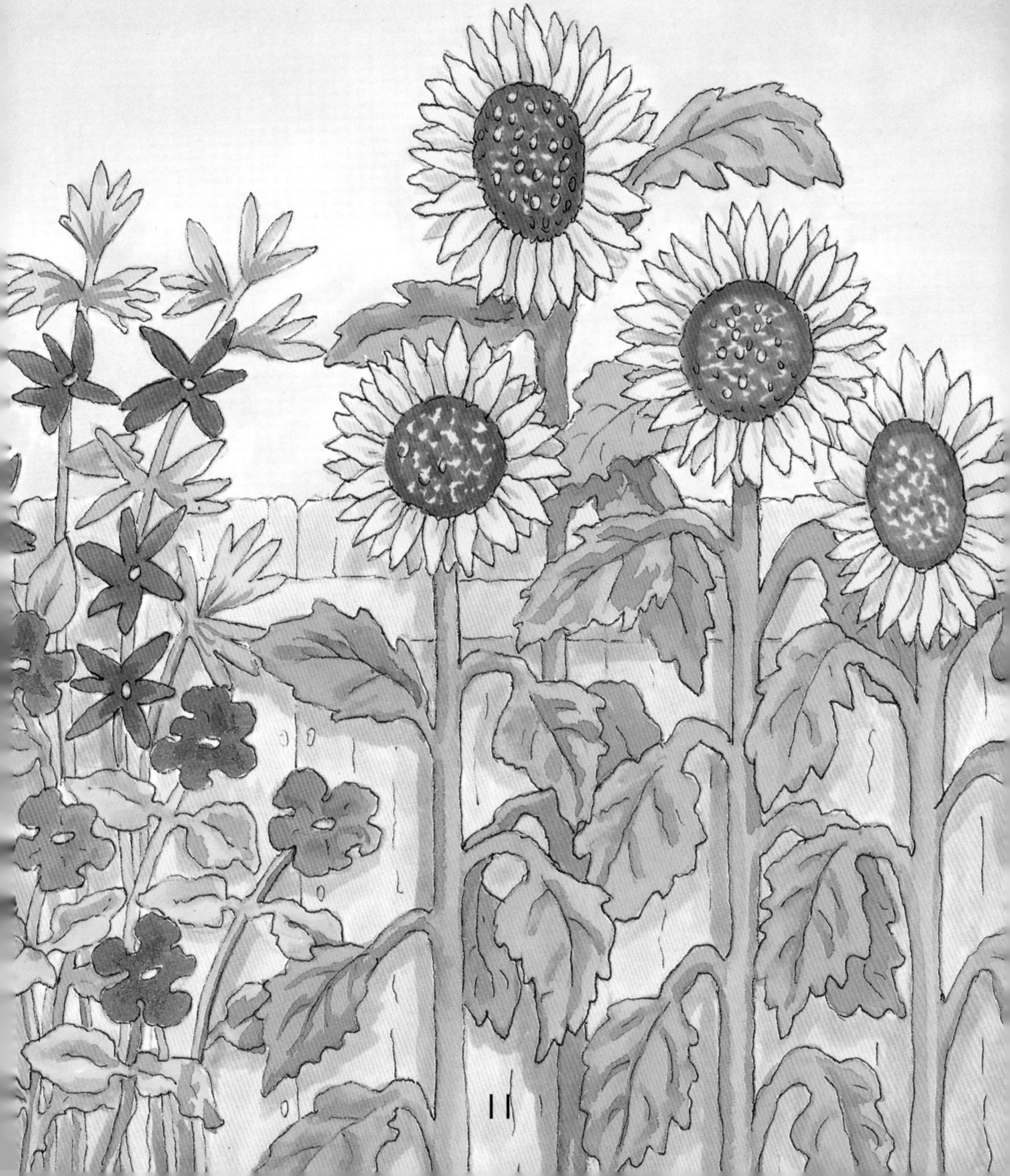

I like trees.

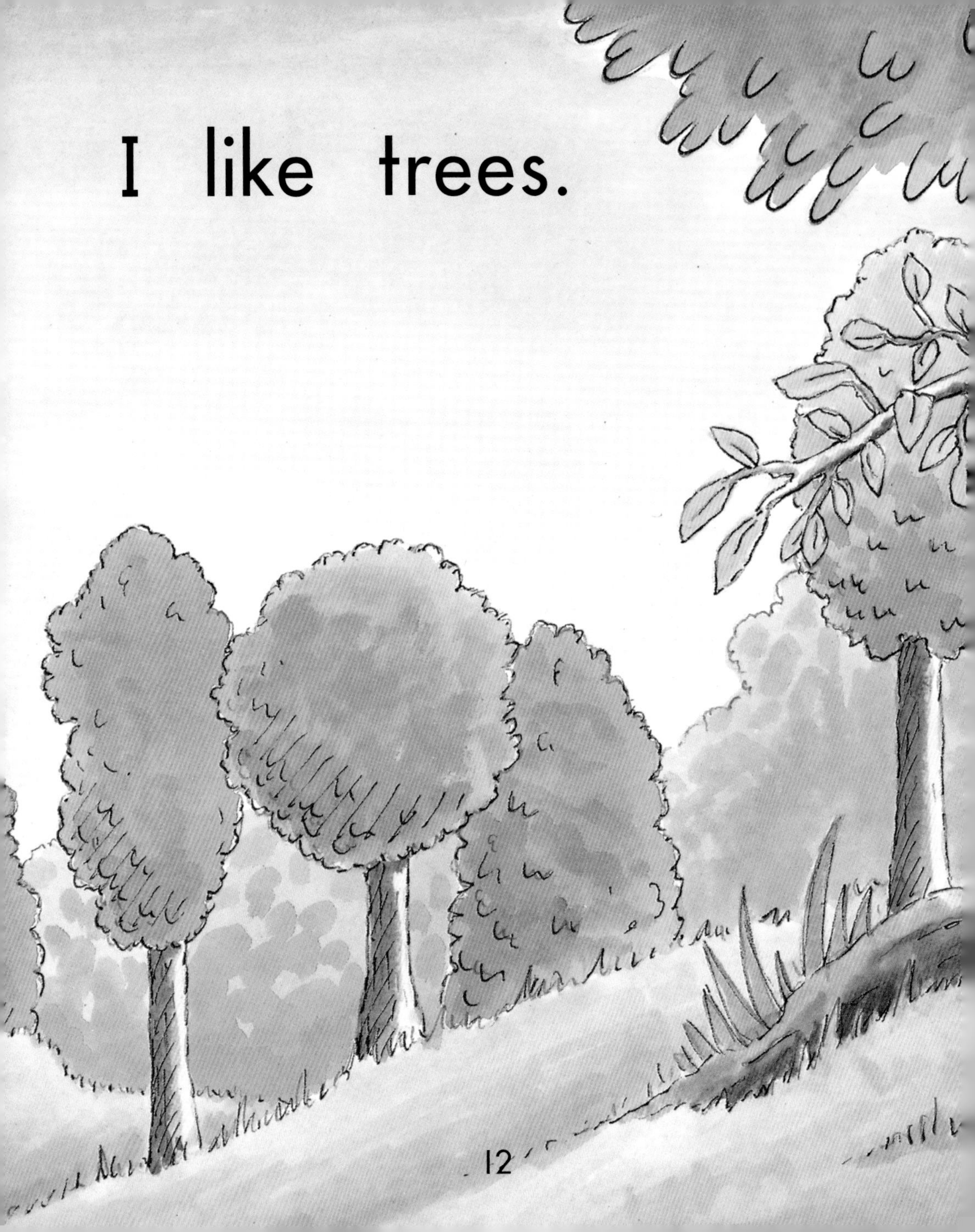

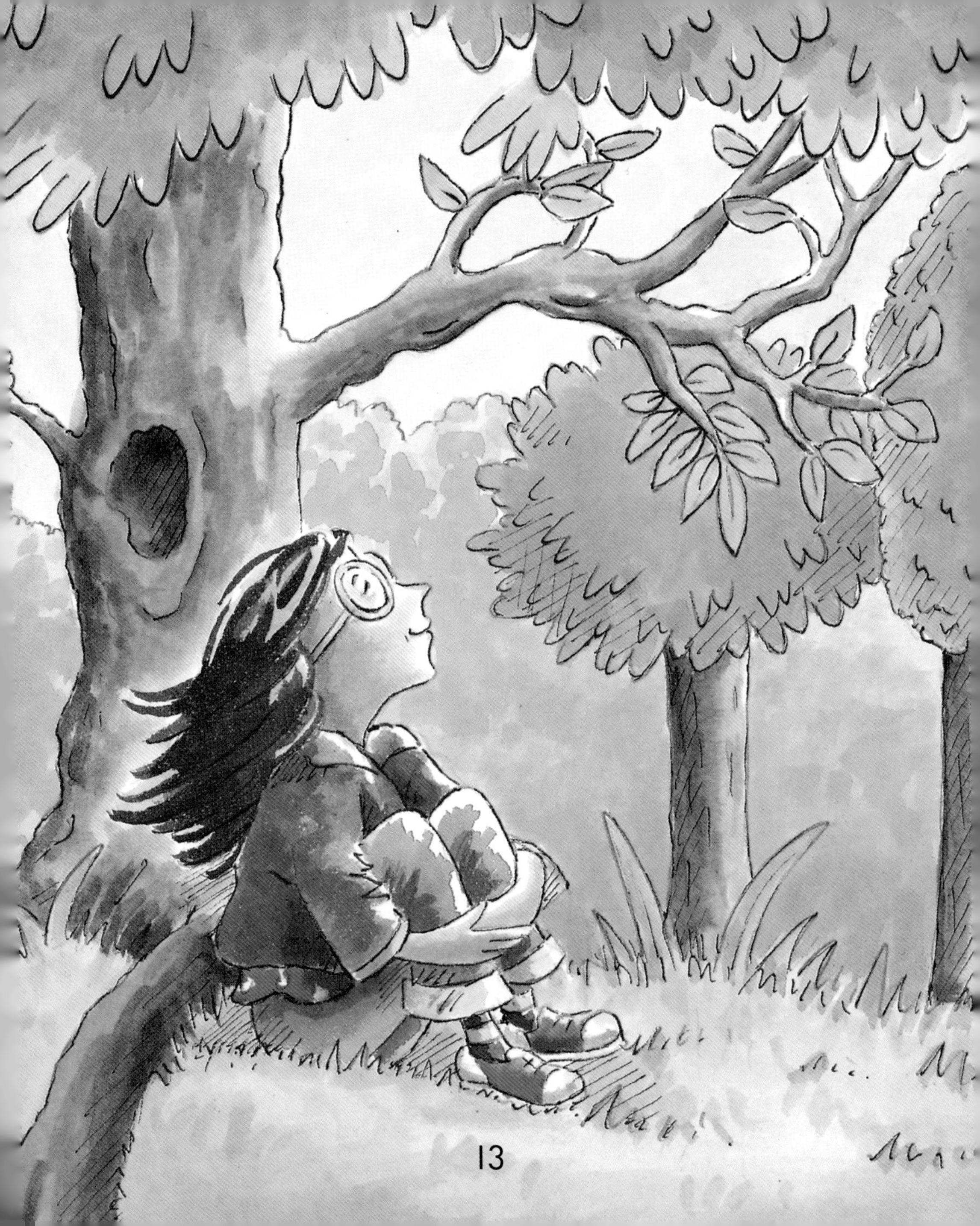

I like you...

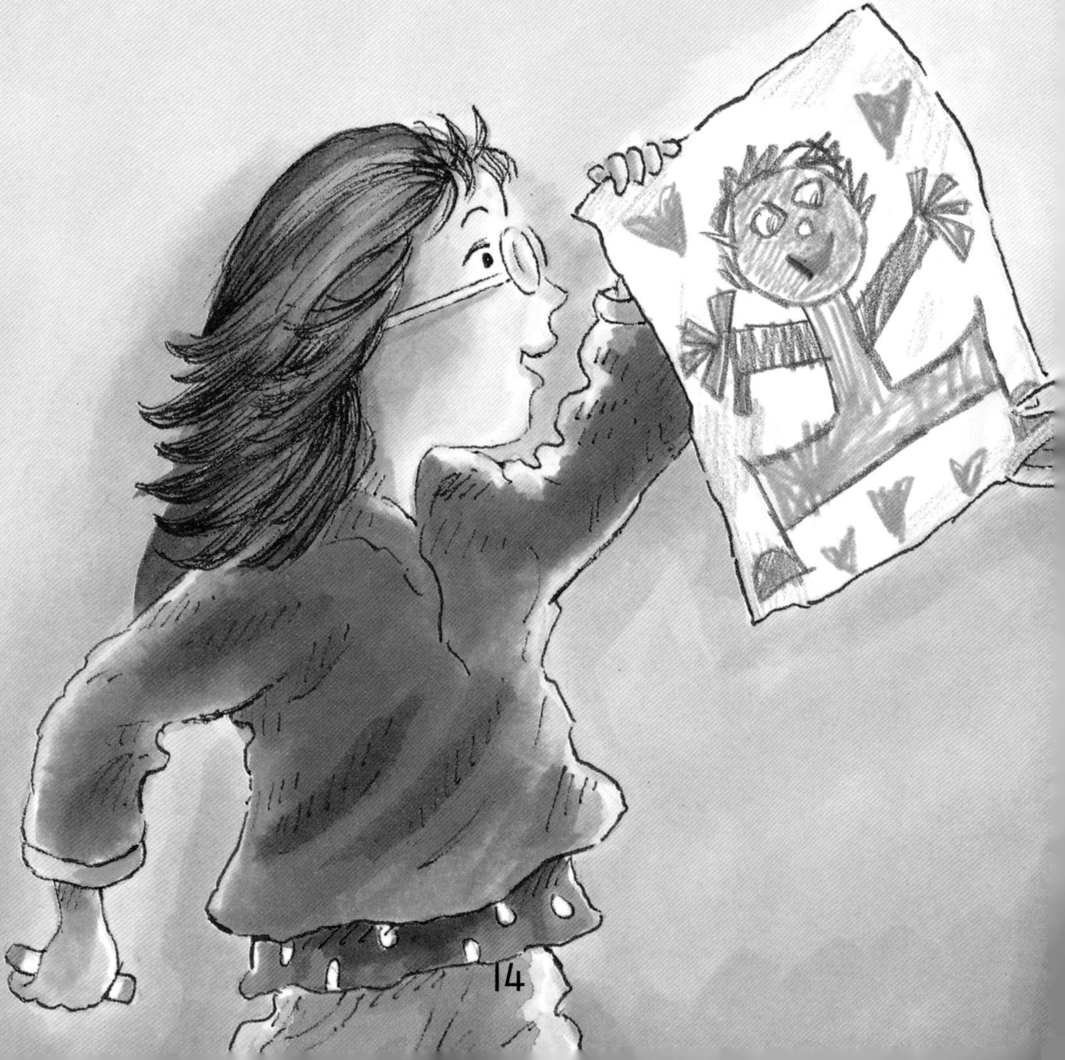

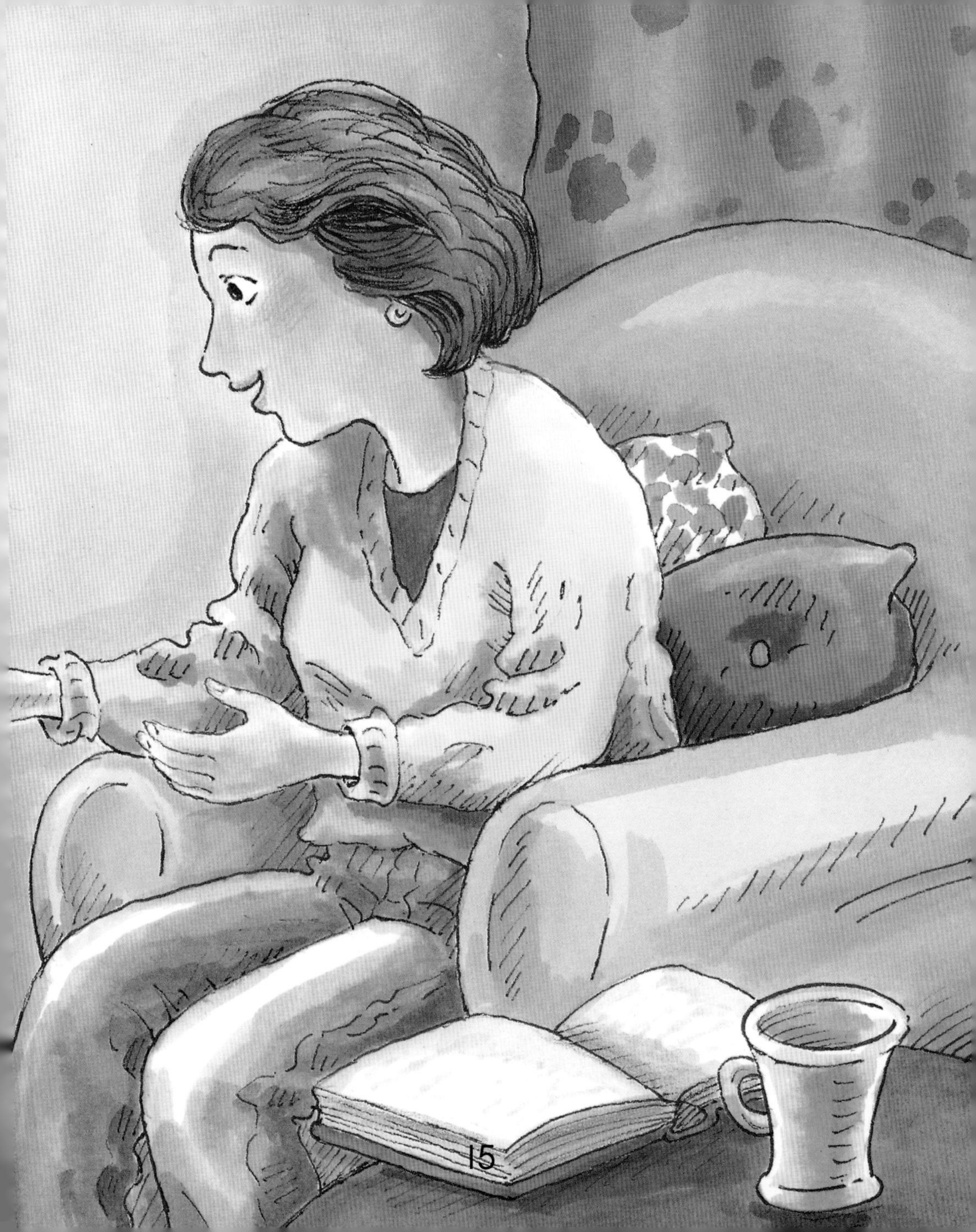

and I like me!

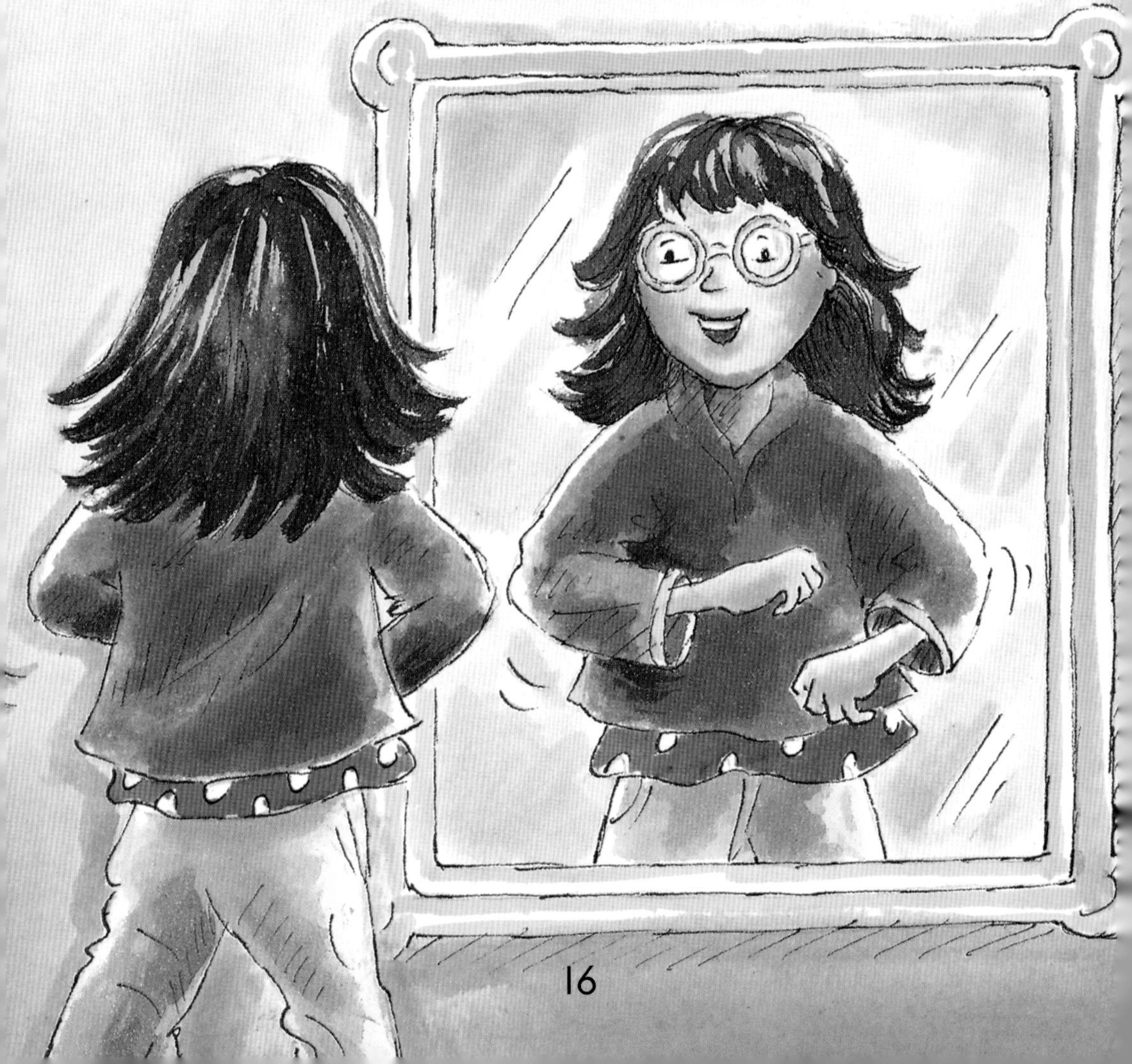